I0465723

The Double Life
of Bitcoin

The Double Life of Bitcoin

All rights reserved.

No part of this book may be reproduced, or stored in a retrieval system, or transmitted in any form or by any means, electronic, mechanical, photocopying, recording, or otherwise, without express written permission of the publisher.

Copyright © 11-30-2024 Steph Wynne All rights reserved-

Cover image by MIDJOURNEY

For more information:

Skinny Books Publishing
PO BOX 34652
Los Angeles, CA 90034

www.skinnybookspublishing.com

ISBN: 9798300346379

Disclaimer

This book is a work of fiction.

Names, characters, places, events, and incidents are either the product of the author's imagination or used fictitiously.

Any resemblance to actual persons, living or dead, or actual events is purely coincidental.

The author makes no representations or warranties with respect to the accuracy or completeness of the content in this book and assumes no liability for any actions taken based on the information contained herein.

This book is intended for entertainment purposes only.

Table of Contents

In the world of Bitcoin, every decision is a gamble—and the stakes are your future.

-Steph Wynne

Prologue

Why I Wrote This Book about Bitcoin

When I wrote my first book, *Gambling on Bitcoin*, July 2021 the world of cryptocurrency was chaotic, technical, and full of hype.

Bitcoin was hailed as the future of money, with bold predictions of $100,000, $200,000, or even a trillion-dollar market cap.

Back then, I tried to break down the complexity of Bitcoin's technology, but the book leaned heavily into the technical side of things—blockchain mechanics, mining, wallets, and the like.

It was informative, but it wasn't exactly an easy read.

Fast forward to 2024, and Bitcoin has finally breached >$90,000. To many, it feels like a vindication of those early predictions.

But I'm still not a fan. Why?

Because Bitcoin, at its core, feels more like gambling than investing. Above ground, it's tied to hype cycles, the whims of influencers, and even the mysterious movements of whales.

And underground, it's a shadowy world of dodging authorities and navigating risks that most people don't fully understand.

If anything, Bitcoin's rise to prominence has only made its true nature more obvious.

It's a double-edged sword: a tool for freedom and a magnet for greed. And somewhere in the middle lies the truth about what Bitcoin really is—a gamble, no matter where you stand.

One thing I can't ignore is how often Bitcoin seems to circle back to Elon Musk. Love him or hate him, Elon's fingerprints are all over the Bitcoin narrative.

In 2021, his tweets could swing the market by billions. Whether he was propping up Dogecoin for laughs or citing environmental concerns to justify Tesla's policies, Elon seemed to hold a kind of invisible leash on Bitcoin.

And maybe now, in 2024, that leash is finally gone. Or maybe he's just lifted the veil, letting Bitcoin find its own way.

The Three Faces of Bitcoin Owners

When I set out to write this book, I wanted to explore Bitcoin in a way that anyone could understand.

Instead of diving into the technical weeds, I chose to focus on the people—the investors, the optimists, and the underground players who keep Bitcoin alive.

In this book, you'll meet three types of Bitcoin owners:

1. Trevor, the Gambler: A middle-aged man chasing quick riches, only to find himself trapped by greed and overconfidence.

2. Janeen, the Cautious Optimist: A young professional who approaches Bitcoin with caution and curiosity, navigating the fine line between luck and strategy.

3. Alex, the Underground Sage: A figure whose embraced the shadows, trading privacy and freedom for the steep cost of staying invisble.

Each story reveals a different side of Bitcoin's double life—above ground and underground, visible and hidden, hopeful and dangerous.

Together, these characters show that Bitcoin isn't just about technology or money. It's about people, choices, and the thin line between risk and reward.

Why You Should Read This Book

I wrote this book for anyone curious about Bitcoin but turned off by all the jargon and technical mumbo-jumbo.

It's not about charts, code, or mining rigs. It's about real people and the decisions they face in the world of cryptocurrency.

Whether you're a complete novice, a cautious investor, or someone who's already dipped a toe into Bitcoin's murky waters, this book will give you a clearer picture of what it means to own Bitcoin—and what it can cost.

So buckle up, and let's explore the double life of Bitcoin together.

It's a ride that's equal parts thrilling, enlightening, and sobering. And maybe, just maybe, it'll help you decide where you stand in this wild, unpredictable world.

Part 1: Trevor's Story – *The Above-Ground Gambler*

The Whisper

Trevor sits at a dimly lit poker table, nursing his third beer. The clink of chips and the low hum of conversation surround him, but he's only half-listening.

Across the table, his friend Greg leans in, his voice hushed but electric: *"Bitcoin. It's like digital gold, man. My buddy just turned fifty grand into a million."*

Trevor shifts uncomfortably in his seat. He doesn't know much about cryptocurrency, but something in Greg's tone grabs his attention—like he's stumbled onto a secret too good to keep.

Trevor forces a chuckle. "Sounds risky," he says, but his curiosity is already piqued.

That night, back at home, Trevor can't sleep. Karen, his wife of 22 years, breathes softly beside him, but his mind races.

He feels the weight of his stagnant savings account, the bills piling up, and the creeping dread of retirement without enough to sustain them. At 50 years old, he's running out of time to build a safety net. Grabbing his phone, he Googles: *"How to buy Bitcoin."*

The First Step

The next morning, Trevor hides his excitement as he pours coffee. Karen stands at the counter, scrolling through her phone. "You're up early," she says without looking up.

"Just wanted to get a jump on the day," Trevor replies, swallowing the lump in his throat. He doesn't mention the hours he spent reading about Bitcoin or the flashy app he downloaded that promises "Crypto made simple!"

By lunchtime, Trevor had transferred $75,000—nearly his entire savings—into the app. A confirmation email pings: *"You've just purchased 1 Bitcoin for $75,000."* He stares at the screen, exhilarated and terrified.

Later, at dinner, Karen chats about their son Ethan's college plans. "He's thinking about UCLA, but he's worried about the cost," she says.

Trevor nods distractedly. "We'll figure it out," he says, though his mind is elsewhere, calculating what Bitcoin's price needs to hit for him to make a significant profit.

The Fever Begins

A week later, Trevor checks his phone and nearly spills his coffee. *Bitcoin hits $95,000!* His $75,000 investment is now worth $95,000—a profit of $20,000 in just days. He feels like a genius.

Karen notices his mood. "You've been in a good mood lately. What's going on?" she asks.

"Just a little investment I made," he says casually, avoiding her eyes.

The next day, Trevor withdraws $10,000 from their joint account and buys more Bitcoin, rationalizing that it's "just a temporary loan" from their emergency fund.

Cracks in the Foundation

The obsession takes hold. Trevor checks Bitcoin prices every 15 minutes, even during family dinner. Karen grows suspicious.

"You're glued to that phone," she says one evening. "What's so important?"

"Work stuff," Trevor lies. He knows she wouldn't understand.

One night, Karen finds a withdrawal notice from their joint account. "Trevor, what's this? You took $10,000 without telling me?"

"It's nothing," he says, brushing it off. "Just an investment. It's already growing."

Karen's face hardens. "This isn't like you. Are you gambling?"

"It's not gambling!" he snaps. "This is smart investing." The edge in his voice silences her, but the tension between them lingers.

The Crash

The high doesn't last. Bitcoin's price skyrockets to $97,000, but Trevor doesn't sell. "It's going to $100K," he tells himself, refusing to lock in his gains.

Then, it happens. Overnight, Bitcoin crashes to $50,000. Trevor wakes up to a sea of red on his app. His $75,000 is now worth $49,277.51.

Panic sets in. He refreshes the app every few seconds, hoping for a rebound.

Karen notices the dark circles under his eyes. "You haven't been yourself lately," she says softly. "What's going on?"

Trevor snaps. "You wouldn't understand! I'm trying to secure our future, not sit back and watch it fall apart!"

Karen steps back, hurt. "You're not securing anything, Trevor. You're risking everything."

The Fallout

Trevor spirals. Determined to recover his losses, he borrows $20,000 against their home equity line of credit to buy more Bitcoin. He tells no one.

Karen discovers the loan documents while cleaning his office. "Are you serious?" she demands, holding the papers in front of him. "You're gambling with our future!"

"It's not gambling!" Trevor yells. "This is how fortunes are made!"

Karen shakes her head, tears in her eyes. "I can't do this anymore, Trevor. You're not the man I married."

That night, she packs a bag and leaves with Ethan to her mother's house.

Rock Bottom

Trevor sits alone in their empty house, staring at the app. Bitcoin now sits at $48,000.

His $75,000 investment is worth less than $27,000. The silence is deafening.

He scrolls through forums looking for answers, but the posts offer no solace: *"Should've sold at the top." "Buy the dip, they said."*

A coworker invites him to a Gamblers Anonymous meeting. At first, Trevor resists, but desperation drives him there.

Sitting in the circle, he listens to others share their stories of ruined lives and shattered families. Finally, he says: "I thought I was investing, but I was just chasing a high."

Picking Up the Pieces

Trevor gets a part-time job at a local hardware store to start paying off his debts. He sells what's left of his Bitcoin at $20,000, taking a brutal loss.

He writes Karen a letter, apologizing and promising to earn back her trust. "I let greed take over," he admits. "But I want to fix what I broke."

Reflection

Months later, Trevor sits on his porch with a cup of coffee, watching the sunrise.

He's learned to find peace in simplicity. While he still reads about Bitcoin, he no longer feels the urge to invest.

"If I ever do it again," he thinks, "it'll be with my eyes wide open—and my family beside me."

Lessons from Trevor

- Don't invest more than you can afford to lose.
- Never let money come before relationships.
- Investing without research or emotional control is just gambling.

The story ends with Trevor journaling his experience, hoping it might help others avoid the same mistakes.

Part 2: Janeen's Story – *The Cautious Optimist*

A Spark of Curiosity

Janeen sits in a bustling coffee shop, her laptop open, half-listening to the hum of conversation around her.

A loud voice from the next table catches her attention: *"Bitcoin's gonna hit $100,000 by the end of the year. It's not a question of if—it's when."*

She glances over, intrigued. A man in a hoodie scrolls through a chart on his phone, gesturing wildly to his friend. Janeen is skeptical, but something about their excitement stays with her.

Later that night, she Googles, *"What is Bitcoin?"* The search returns pages of results: articles, forums, YouTube videos.

She clicks on one titled, *"Bitcoin: The Future of Money or a Total Scam?"* The host breaks down Bitcoin's basics—digital currency, blockchain, mining—but what grabs her attention is its wild price swings.

She wonders if this is just gambling dressed up in tech jargon.

The First Step

Over the next week, Janeen dives deeper.

She watches late-night videos about Bitcoin's history, from its mysterious creation by "Satoshi Nakamoto" to its meteoric rise and infamous crashes.

She learns about the whales—players who own vast amounts of Bitcoin and can manipulate the market.

After days of research, she sets up an account on a well-reviewed exchange.

Unlike Trevor, she's cautious, depositing only $200, an amount she's prepared to lose. She buys a fraction of a Bitcoin at $62,000.

When the confirmation email arrives, she feels a mix of excitement and unease.

Learning the Game

Janeen's $200 turns into $250 within a week as Bitcoin climbs to $65,000.

"Not bad," she thinks, but she remembers the videos warning about greed.

She begins following forums where traders discuss market trends.

One post catches her eye, from a user named "AnonCryptoSage":

"The bait is shiny. But the deeper you go, the darker it gets. Whales don't lose—small fish do."

Intrigued, Janeen replies, asking what the user means. They respond: *"Watch the wallets. When whales move, prices dive."*

She spends hours digging into blockchain analysis, discovering tools that track large Bitcoin transactions.

It feels like a puzzle, and she loves puzzles.

The Fever (Controlled)

Bitcoin hits $67,000, and Janeen's initial investment has grown to $280.

Her coworkers tease her at lunch: "Careful, Janeen, you'll be a crypto bro soon!"

She laughs but doesn't tell them how much time she spends analyzing charts after work.

One evening, she notices an unusual transaction: a whale moves 100,000 Bitcoin to an exchange.

Remembering AnonCryptoSage's advice, she sells her Bitcoin locking in a modest profit.

Days later, Bitcoin crashed to $43,000. Janeen feels relief but also guilt. "Was I lucky?" she wonders, or did her research actually pay off?

The Whisper Underground

Her success emboldens her. She messages AnonCryptoSage to thank them for their advice.

Their reply is enigmatic:*"Above ground, you're bait. Below, you're invisible. Ready to dive deeper?"*

Curious, Janeen asks what they mean. They send her a link to a private forum.

It's a world she didn't know existed—discussions about privacy wallets, decentralized exchanges, and coins designed to hide transactions.

She reads stories of people who use Bitcoin to escape oppressive governments or bypass financial systems.

It's fascinating, but there's an edge of danger. One post warns: *"The underground isn't for the faint of heart. It's a tool, not a game."*

The Crossroads

Janeen begins experimenting.

She moves a small portion of her profits into Monero, a privacy coin. She learns how to use decentralized exchanges, where there's no middleman, just peer-to-peer transactions.

But she also feels the tension. "Why hide?" she wonders. "I'm not doing anything illegal."

Yet the allure of the underground world—the control, the anonymity—pulls at her.

Her parents, retired teachers, ask her about Bitcoin at Sunday dinner.

"It's interesting," she says vaguely. She doesn't mention the underground forums or the encrypted messages she now exchanges with AnonCryptoSage.

A Close Call

One day, Janeen receives a frantic message on the forum: *"IRS just flagged my account for unreported Bitcoin gains.*

They're tracking everything above ground now. Get out while you can!"

Her heart races. She hasn't done anything wrong, but she knows her transactions are visible on the blockchain.

She immediately moves her remaining Bitcoin to a private wallet, following advice from the forum.

That night, she dreams of being audited, her accounts frozen, her name in the headlines. She wakes up in a cold sweat, questioning whether this new world is worth the risk.

Into the Shadows

Janeen decides to dive deeper. With guidance from AnonCryptoSage, she sets up a hardware wallet and secures her keys offline.

She learns about mixers—tools that anonymize Bitcoin transactions by pooling and redistributing funds.

But the underground isn't all freedom. She encounters scams, losing a small portion of her Monero in a fraudulent transaction. "A cheap lesson," AnonCryptoSage tells her. "The underground teaches fast."

The Shift

Months later, Janeen feels like a different person. She's more cautious, more private.

She no longer tells her coworkers about her Bitcoin holdings. Her profits are modest, but she values her independence more than the money.

Her biggest challenge is reconciling her new life with her relationships.

She starts pulling back from friends who ask too many questions. "It's better this way," she tells herself, though she misses the connection.

The Choice

AnonCryptoSage invites Janeen to join a larger underground network—a group dedicated to building entirely decentralized systems.

Janeen hesitates. She enjoys the control and privacy of the underground but isn't sure she wants to disappear completely.

n the end, she declines. Instead, she begins teaching others how to invest cautiously, balancing above-ground visibility with underground safety.

"You don't have to pick one world or the other," she tells her small but growing audience.

As she logs off the forum for the last time, she receives a final message from AnonCryptoSage:

"Freedom is knowing you can choose."

Part 3: Alex's Story – *The Underground Sage*

The Phantom Begins

Alex watches the Bitcoin price tick upward on a clunky, outdated laptop in a cramped, dimly lit apartment.

A faint hum from a nearby air conditioner fills the silence. The headlines scream about Bitcoin hitting $90,000, and social media is ablaze with euphoric investors.

Alex feels none of their excitement.

This isn't a celebration—it's a warning. When the masses rush in, the predators follow.

Opening an encrypted chat on a private forum, Alex types: *"The bait is shiny. But the deeper you go, the darker it gets."*

This is the kind of message Alex lives for—not advice, but a breadcrumb for the curious.

A Long Road to the Shadows

Alex wasn't always underground. Years ago, he was just another tech worker, managing servers for a midsized corporation.

The pay was decent, the benefits solid, but the work felt hollow.

The turning point came when Alex read about a whistleblower who exposed mass surveillance programs.

The article detailed how governments tracked every click, message, and transaction.

It wasn't paranoia—it was fact. Alex's disillusionment grew into obsession.

He started experimenting with Bitcoin, drawn by its promise of anonymity and independence.

But even then, the cracks showed. Every transaction was logged on a public ledger, visible to anyone who cared to look.

"This isn't privacy," Alex muttered one night, staring at their wallet's transaction history. "It's a trap for the naïve."

So Alex went deeper—privacy coins, mixers, and decentralized exchanges became their tools of choice.

The deeper he went, the harder it was to come back.

The Tools of the Trade

Alex keeps no digital footprints. His phone is a burner. His laptop runs on a privacy-focused operating system.

Every transaction is routed through Tor, and their funds are split across wallets no one else can trace.

The cost of such precautions is steep. Alex hasn't seen his family in years—too many questions, too many risks.

Relationships are a luxury he can't afford. "Freedom comes at a price," Alex often tells himself, though he rarely admits how much it hurts.

On the forums, Alex becomes a myth. His advice is cryptic but compelling, laced with warnings about greed and carelessness.

When Janeen's message pops up—eager, polite, yet cautious—Alex hesitates before responding. He's helped many before, but not all have listened.

The Philosophy of Shadows

One night, Alex sits at his desk, staring at the glowing screen. The latest forum thread is buzzing: *"Bitcoin's future: Revolution or ruin?"*

Alex replies with a single sentence: *"Bitcoin isn't a revolution. It's a tool. Use it wisely, or it will use you."*

The post gets dozens of replies. Some call Alex a pessimist; others hail him as a prophet. Alex doesn't care for the labels.

His philosophy is simple: privacy isn't about hiding—it's about control.

A memory surfaces—an old friend who stayed above ground, investing heavily in Bitcoin during a bull run.

When the market crashed, the friend panicked, sold everything, and was later flagged by the IRS for failing to report gains.

Alex warned them, but his friend didn't listen.

That was the day Alex stopped offering advice and started offering warnings.

The Janeen Connection

Janeen's cautious messages intrigue Alex. She isn't like most above-ground investors.

She asks the right questions, listens more than she speaks, and seems genuinely interested in learning, not just profiting.

Over weeks, Alex guides her into the underground world—starting small, teaching her about privacy wallets and decentralized exchanges.

But Alex notices something unusual about Janeen: she isn't entirely comfortable in the shadows.

One day, she asks, *"Why do you stay underground? Isn't it lonely?"*

Alex pauses before typing back: *"Loneliness is better than chains."*

The Cost of Freedom

Alex rarely thinks about the price of his lifestyle, but Janeen's question lingers.

Freedom, they've learned, is a double-edged sword. It offers independence but demands isolation.

Years ago, Alex cut ties with everyone who might compromise his anonymity. Family birthdays became distant memories.

Old friendships faded into silence. Even casual outings felt like risks—not worth the exposure.

But Alex has also seen the price others pay above ground: frozen accounts, crushing debts, lives destroyed by reckless investments or regulatory crackdowns.

He thinks of Trevor—a gambler who ignored every warning.

"Better to be lonely than controlled," Alex mutters, though the words feel hollow.

A Warning Ignored

The forum buzzes with rumors of a coming crash.

Whales are moving massive amounts of Bitcoin to exchanges, a clear sign they're preparing to sell.

Alex posts a warning:*"The sharks are circling. Time to leave the water."*

But the response is mixed. Some heed the advice, selling their Bitcoin or moving funds to private wallets.

Others dismiss Alex as a doomsayer.

Janeen sends a private message: *"Thanks for the tip. I cashed out just in time."*

Alex feels a rare flicker of satisfaction. At least one person listened.

The Shadows Deepen

Bitcoin crashes to $64,000, then $59,000. The forums erupt with panic.

One user posts: *"The IRS flagged my account for unreported gains. They froze everything."*

Alex replies with their usual cryptic tone: *"Above ground, they watch everything. Underground, they can't see you."*

But Alex knows the underground isn't perfect. Scammers lurk everywhere, and even privacy tools have weaknesses.

One misstep, and everything can unravel.

The Final Message

Janeen sends another message, asking for advice on going deeper into the underground. But Alex senses her hesitation.

She's not like them—she values connection and community, things the underground rarely allows.

Alex types back: *"Freedom is knowing when to stop. You don't have to disappear to stay safe."*

For the first time, Alex considers whether he's gone too far.

The Price of Independence

Months later, Alex shuts down his forum account, leaving behind a final post: *"Freedom isn't in the money. It's in the choices you make. Stay vigilant."*

He packs his belongings into a single bag and moves to a new city, restarting under a new identity.

For Alex, the journey never ends. The underground isn't a destination—it's a way of life, and one they've chosen to embrace despite its cost.

As he logs off for the last time, Alex feels a rare pang of longing for a simpler world—one where freedom didn't require so many sacrifices.

But he pushed the thought away.

In the shadows, there's no room for regret.

Bitcoin: Above Ground vs. Underground

Bitcoin above ground is a gamble.

The visible, regulated world of cryptocurrency offers the illusion of safety, but it's rife with manipulation, volatility, and the ever-present eye of authorities.

For many, it's a game of chance where luck often outweighs skill.

The underground, on the other hand, offers anonymity and independence, but it's not a sanctuary—it's a battleground.

Operating underground requires knowledge, resources, and constant vigilance. Privacy tools, decentralized exchanges, and mixers can shield you from prying eyes, but they come with steep costs, both financial and emotional.

It's not for everyone.

The Price of the Underground

Returning to the underground today feels different than it did in the early days of Bitcoin.

The barriers to entry are higher, both in complexity and cost. Privacy coins like Monero, secure wallets, and decentralized tools often require significant investments of time and money. And even then, the risks remain: scams, vulnerabilities, and the loneliness of living in a world where trust is scarce.

For someone who's tasted both worlds, like Alex, the underground can feel like the last bastion of freedom—but it's an expensive one.

And for those like Janeen, who value connection and balance, the underground might feel like too high a price to pay.

Final Thougnts

Bitcoin's double life is both its greatest strength and its biggest flaw.

Above ground, it's a gamble—exciting, dangerous, and often devastating.

Underground, it's a labyrinth—difficult to navigate and increasingly out of reach for the average person.

As someone who sees the appeal of returning underground, I recognize the challenges. It's not just about money—it's about the willingness to sacrifice convenience, relationships, and simplicity for a fleeting sense of control.

The question is: how much are you willing to pay for freedom?

For some, the answer will always be "whatever it takes."

For others, the cost will feel too high.

And for those caught in between, like Trevor, Janeen, and Alex, Bitcoin will remain what it has always been—a double-edged sword, offering hope, freedom, and danger in equal measure.

The double life of Bitcoin isn't just about money. It's about choices.

And those choices, ultimately, define who you are and where you stand in a world that's constantly shifting between the visible and the invisible.

About The Author Steph Wynne

I've been blessed to have written 20 (skinny books for a fast read) on various subjects!

I just love to read and write!

It hasn't always been that way. As I got older I realized that I was a "learner." With learning came reading and then writing!

Now I can't stop! If I could have a wish it would be to have my words read 100 years from now!

I live in Los Angeles, California and you can find my books here www.skinnybookspublishing.com or on Amazon!

Thank you!

Steph

www.ingramcontent.com/pod-product-compliance
Lightning Source LLC
Chambersburg PA
CBHW070428240526
45472CB00020B/1649